Pimp My Walker

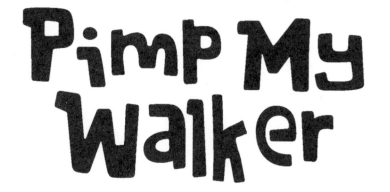

Pimp My Walker

The Official Book of Old Age Haiku

MIKE SLOSBERG

BUNKER HILL PUBLISHING

www.bunkerhillpublishing.com

First published in 2007
by Bunker Hill Publishing Inc.
285 River Road, Piermont
New Hampshire 03779, USA

10 9 8 7 6 5 4 3 2 1

Text and illustrations copyright © Mike Slosberg

Library of Congress Control Number: 2007926765

ISBN 9781593730635

Designed by Louise Millar

Printed in China by Jade Productions Ltd

Introduction

Old age isn't always wonderful, but the alternative really sucks!

Maneuvering through the years is a lot like driving cross-country on secondary roads. There are the occasional potholes, flat tires, bad food and traffic jams.

And, depending on any given moment in time, your journey can be funny, sad, ironic, painful, satisfying, frustrating and challenging.

But, regardless, we all wish for a long trip, one hopefully filled with laughter...even if the humor is occasionally at our own expense.

It reminds me of the joke about two elderly women recently returned from a weeklong cruise. The first lady laments about the terrible food. Her friend agrees the food was truly disgusting and adds, that to make matters worse, the portions were way too...small!

So even if life is, at times, like a bad meal, we still want the portions to be as large as possible.

Pimp My Walker is brimming with 73 Haiku poems that celebrate the irony, the humor, the rewards and, yes, the occasional unhappy aspects of aging.

For example, take your aging bladder problems. A tragedy? It all depends, you should pardon the pun.

> I'm at the fourth tee
> When my bladder signals: Full.
> I shoot for the rough.

And what about that slowly diminishing libido?

> I can remember
> When sex was better than food.
> Now vice is versa

In a sense, *Pimp My Walker* is an owner's manual for aging with humor. So whether you just turned 40 or are slipping to the far side of 80, be thankful for laughter.

At best, it will keep you youthful; at worst, it's good for the digestion.

Enjoy!

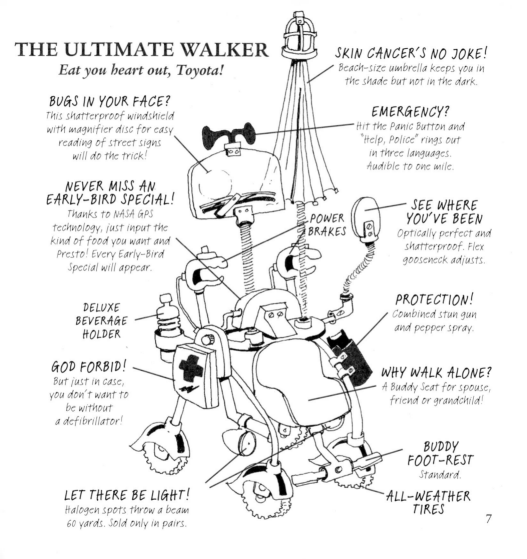

THE ULTIMATE WALKER
Eat you heart out, Toyota!

SKIN CANCER'S NO JOKE!
Beach-size umbrella keeps you in the shade but not in the dark.

BUGS IN YOUR FACE?
This shatterproof windshield with magnifier disc for easy reading of street signs will do the trick!

EMERGENCY?
Hit the Panic Button and "Help, Police" rings out in three languages. Audible to one mile.

NEVER MISS AN EARLY-BIRD SPECIAL!
Thanks to NASA GPS technology, just input the kind of food you want and Presto! Every Early-Bird Special will appear.

POWER BRAKES

SEE WHERE YOU'VE BEEN
Optically perfect and shatterproof. Flex gooseneck adjusts.

DELUXE BEVERAGE HOLDER

PROTECTION!
Combined stun gun and pepper spray.

GOD FORBID!
But just in case, you don't want to be without a defibrillator!

WHY WALK ALONE?
A Buddy Seat for spouse, friend or grandchild!

BUDDY FOOT-REST
Standard.

LET THERE BE LIGHT!
Halogen spots throw a beam 60 yards. Sold only in pairs.

ALL-WEATHER TIRES

7

1

Growing old with style

Means being picky about

One's brand of walker

2

Not much hair on top
Could cut it short but instead
Choose a comb over

3

My painful back could
Be a sign of early death
An Aspirin might help

4

I can remember

When sex was better than food

Now vice is versa

5

The dentist I see
Is a lot younger than some
Of my gold inlays

6

My wife and I speak
In sentences that start with
"What? What did you say?"

7

China vacation
Breakfasting on the Yangtze
Yearning for Zabars

8

Legs inside tubes of
Stretch nylon, knee-to-toe, my
Sole means of support

9

She's eating a plum
Parted red lips. Pink, wet tongue.
And I'm thinking food?

10

It's just our first date
She offers me super sex.
I opt for the soup

19

11

Backs of my hands are
Liver-spot-mottled just like
Army camouflage

12

Once her breasts faced up,
I clearly recall. Sadly,
Gravity kicked-in

13

Had two Martinis
Woke up at three with chest pains
A death by reflux?

14

I've a replaced hip
My second, and a new knee
Could God do better?

"You know I was watching that!
Now you're just sneezing on purpose."

15

I've a pacemaker
But whenever I sneeze hard
The channel changes.

16

I'm at the fourth tee
When my bladder signals: Full.
I shoot for the rough.

17

We mock what we are
To be, until we ourselves
Become the to-be

18

Friends in hospitals
Mean a fortune in cab fares
Going to, and fro

19

Popped a hernia
Should I go under the knife?
Or just truss in God?

"You can't see my grandson until he cries simply because I've forgotten where I put him."

20

Grandkids are a joy
Play a while, and hand them back
Just like a Hertz car

21

High school reunion
Everyone looks so ancient
Except yours truly

22

Love retirement:
Going to movies, alone
In the afternoon

23

Up each morning, with
nothing to do, but by day's end
haven't done it all

24

My memory's lost
At my age, there's not enough
Time, to get it back

25

Had sex last night, with
A youngster of 80. At
Least...I hope I did.

37

26

My meds are lovely
They resemble precious gems
Which — price-wise — they are

27

I wake up and pee.
Still in my bed when I do
Now, that's a problem

28

Went to a picnic
Corn-on-the-cob looked great...but
I'd left my teeth home.

29

Dining well at four
Early Birds end their days with
A smile and a Burp!

"Physically my doctor says I'm good for 20 more years. Financially my accountant says I'll be lucky to last ten."

30

Money's got to last
As long as me. But if it
Doesn't...do I die?

31

I've a new best friend
Because the old best-one died
Survivors move up

32

Those varicose veins
On my legs, sort of look like
A Jackson Pollock

33

Heart needs a new valve
If they get it from a pig
I won't be Kosher!

34

Gorgeous girl drops keys
I stoop quickly to grab them.
A painful mistake

35

I want cremation
Ashes, out of my wife's reach
On top of the fridge?

*He always wanted to take it all with him. So I calculated
his net worth and put a check for that amount in the coffin.*

36

We've stopped arguing.
Not a good sign, since conflict
Helps circulation.

37

The young bride is half
His age. It's like having a
New car and no gas

38

Wife says you can't hear!
Doc says I've got SHL
Spousal Hearing Loss

39

She gets hot flashes.
He sweats in the dark. Could roast
A few marshmallows?

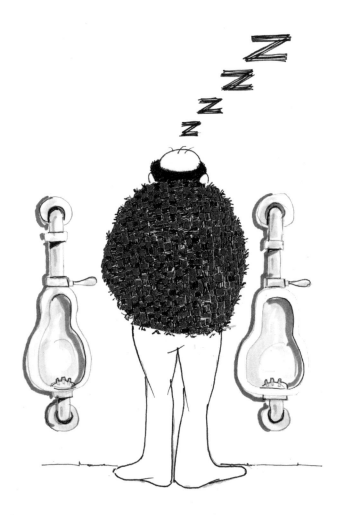

40

Pass wind with great care
Take every bathroom break, and
Ignore no hard on

41

My ménage à trois:
A sleeping pill, me and a
Hot water bottle

42

Dating a young gal
My kids are beside themselves
Fearing for their trust

43

Seen and done it all.
My only problem is this:
Who can remember?

44

I wear diapers.
It controls most excess leaks
Eat your heart out Bush

45

My grandson and I
Have something big in common.
We both wear Pampers

"Who changes your diapers, Pop-Pop"

46

If a tree falls in
the forest, and my wife's not
there, am I still wrong?

47

Bridal registry
at a pharmacy makes sense
when you are my age

48

Doggie steps are cool
Helps old pets climb into bed
Perfect now, for me

49

Could Alzheimer's be
God's sly way of letting us
laugh at our old jokes

"I filled it with Pop's favorite prescriptions!"

50

Christmas here again
My stocking's hung with care but...
Now it's support hose

51

I was a great cook.
Famous for my gourmet meals
Now, I burn the toast

52

Now that I go to
Movies alone, I'm eating
A lot more popcorn

53

My grandson is five
He asked me about Lincoln
As if I knew him

54

I email people
I've not met, because on-line
I'm any age I want

55

Sailing on cruise ship.
Bored to distraction. Eating
Continuously

56

Friends...those still alive
...Live in Florida, which I
Call, God's waiting room

57

My backhand was strong
But now, with the new hip, must
Depend on drop-shots

58

HDL is high
LDL is low. All's well
With the world. Thank God.

59

My blood pressure is
Like a Yo-Yo. Doc suggests
Doing "walk-the-dog"

60

Now that my wife's gone
Friends try hard to fix me up
Thinking I'm broken

"*I'm delighted you've found a retirement hobby but if it doesn't work out, promise you won't cut your ear off.*"

61

Wake up with back pain
Takes all day to walk upright
Just in time for bed

62

Mutters to himself,
Like me...walking along, but
He's on a cell phone

63

Laptop's a blessing
Tons of memory, and more!
I play solitaire

64

I check on my stocks
Marvel at their ups and downs
I should be so agile.

65

Got a computer
Can't use it yet, but it looks
Good on the table

66

A friend broke her hip

Now everyone I know has

At least one new part

67

Present from my son.
He says it's a Blackberry.
Rather have ripe peach.

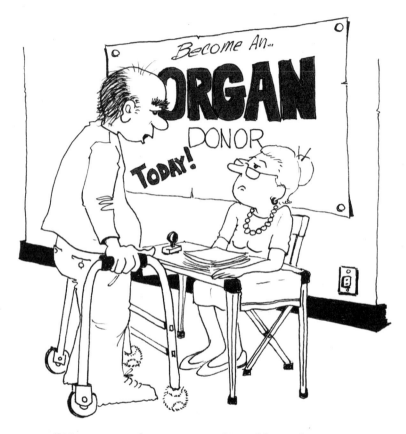

"Listen, sweetheart, I got a big, old Wurlitzer at home and if you can get it out, it's all yours!"

68

Donate an organ?
None of mine work anyway.
So what's the point?

69

Cremation might work.
Resting in a fancy urn
Seems rather pleasant.

7o

Memory is shot.
My keys, wallet and glasses
Elude me, always

71

I'm incontinent.
That is, in America
And not traveling.

"I clearly recall parking by an even number and a vowel."

72

A second marriage
Is often better than first.
Should start with latter

73

Love "tricked-out" cars but
I'm too frail to drive so I'll
Just pimp my walker

Afterword

Now It's Your Turn!

Haiku is a very interesting form of Japanese poetry.

It's also a form of poetry that's fun to play around with and gives one a quick and easy outlet for feelings, attitudes, foibles and emotions.

Writing Haiku is quite simple. In a way it's sort of like doing a little crossword puzzle.

Here's what Haiku is: A verse that's made up of 17 syllables, chopped into three lines.

First line -- with a total of five syllables.
Second line -- with a total of seven syllables.
Third line -- with a total of five syllables.

So give it a try.
There's very little to lose.
(Fill in the last line)

It's that simple

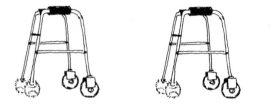
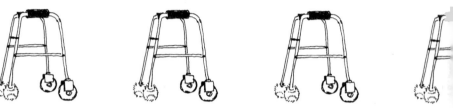